Contents

An old, old game................ 2
Roman football................. 4
Football in the streets......... 6
Ban football................... 8
Village football............... 10
Football in America........... 12
Two different games.......... 14
Rugby and soccer............. 16
Football clubs................ 20
Football all over the world..... 22
Index......................... 24

An old, old game

Everyone knows what football is. But did you know that football is a very old game? How old is it? No one knows!

Good left foot!

3

Roman football

Did you know that the Romans played football? The Romans did not have goal posts. They had goal lines. They used their hands and feet to get the ball over the line.

"Go! Go! Go!"

"Help!"

"Ow!"

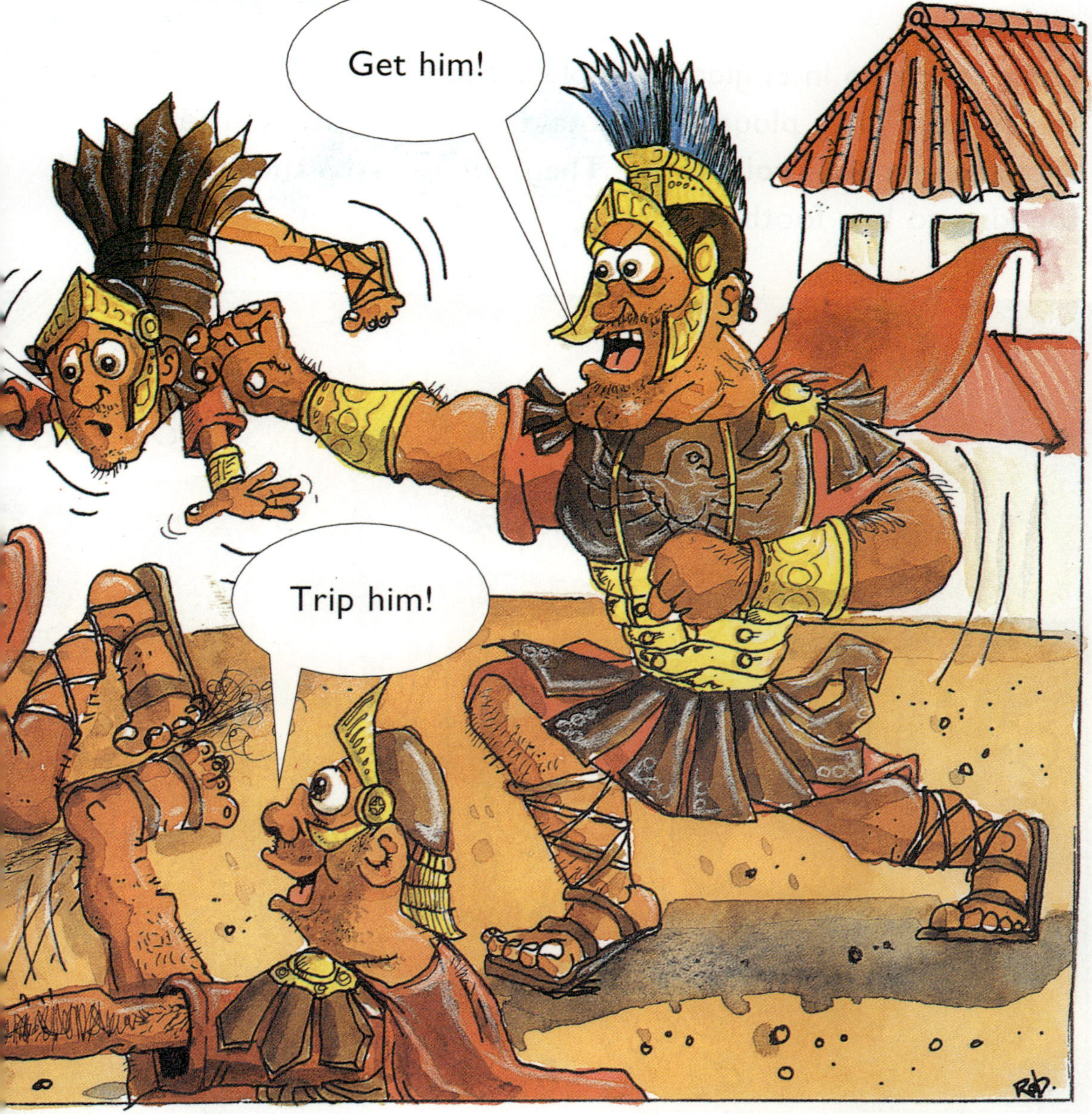
Get him!
Trip him!

Football in the streets

Long, long ago in England, people played football. They played in the streets. They played all around shops and stalls. The shopkeepers got really cross. They got so cross that they asked the king to ban football.

"Go away!"

"Run! Run!"

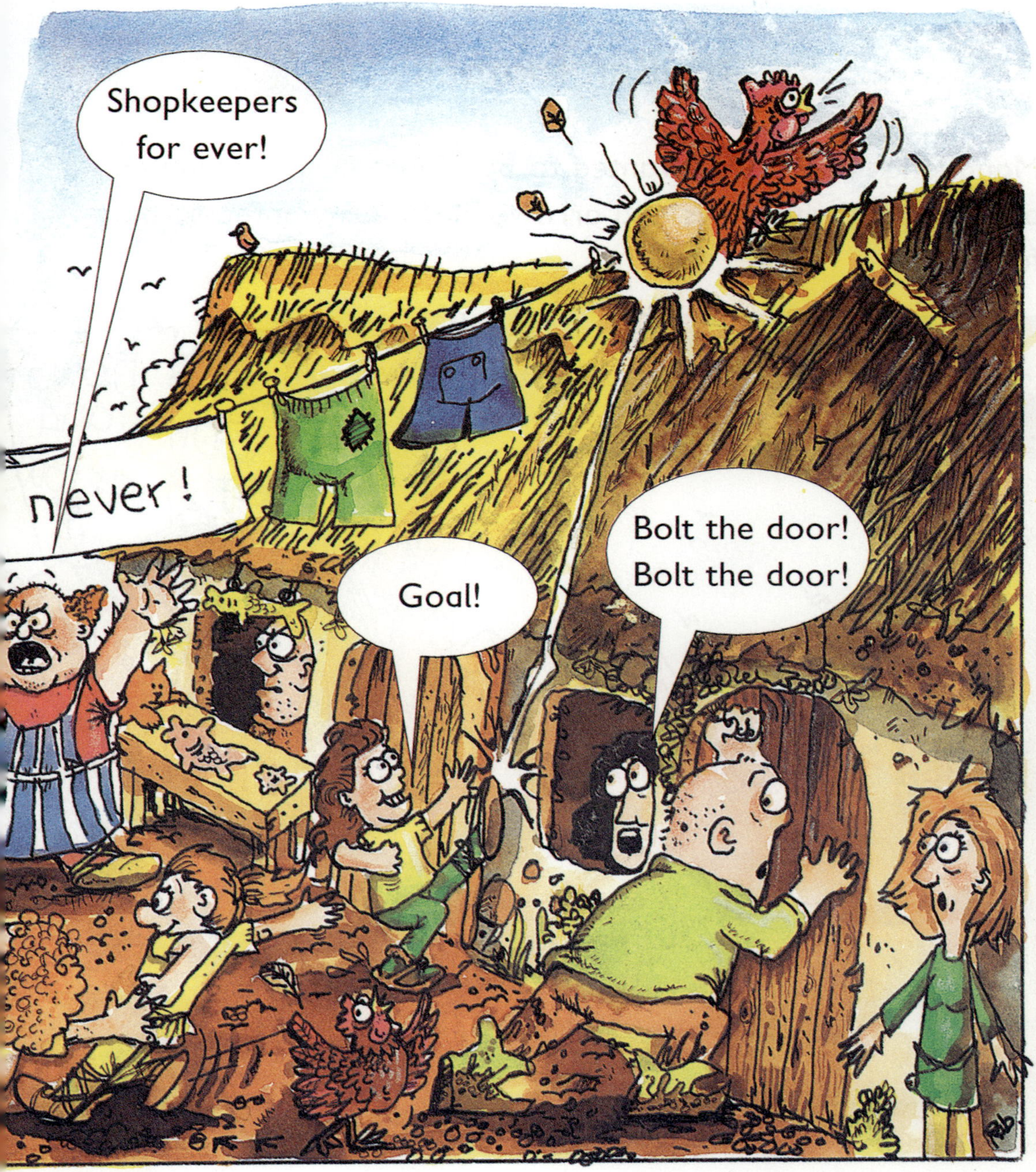
Shopkeepers for ever!
never!
Goal!
Bolt the door! Bolt the door!

Ban football

Many kings of England wanted to ban football. They wanted boys to play with bows and arrows. But boys wanted to play football.

Read this!
No football
King Henry
Give me that ball!
Put footballs here
No! I want a football!

Village football

Long ago in England, there was a game like a really big football game. It was called village football. You had to get the football from one village to the next. It was dangerous because there were no rules. You could get hurt playing village football. Some people were even killed!

I've got the ball!

Help! I can't swim!

"Get off my head!"

"Ow!"

Football in America

People played football in America, too. There were lots and lots of people on each team. The goals were over a kilometre wide. The rules were not like today's football rules. You could hit, kick and jump on other players.

Help! I can't swim!

"Come down here! Don't be a baby!"

"No way!"

"Ow!"

Two different games

For a long time, there were two different kinds of ball. Each had a different shape. Each kind of game had different rules. The two main kinds of game were played by schools and by clubs.

15

Rugby and soccer

In 1896, the football games played in schools and clubs were called different names. They were called rugby and soccer. Soccer is also called football.

"We don't like your rules!"

"Ow!"

"Soccer for ever!"

17

Rugby and football had very different rules. Here are the two sets of rules they had then.

Rugby
1 You can catch the ball and run with it.
2 You can trip up the player with the ball.
3 It is a goal when the ball goes over the bar.
4 The ball does not have to be round.

Football
1 You can stop the ball with your hand but you cannot run with it.
2 You can jump at the player with the ball but you can't kick, trip or grab him.
3 It is a goal when the ball goes inside the posts and under the bar.
4 The ball is round.

It's OK – it's in the new rules!

Football clubs

By 1885, there were many football clubs in England and Scotland. Clubs began to pay people to play for them. Soon you had to pay the club if you wanted to see the game.

Pay here! Pay here!

Two, please.

Thanks, Dad!

Oops!

21

Football all over the world

In the 1880s, football clubs from England and Scotland went to play all over the world. Lots of people went to see them play. They liked what they saw! So all over the world, people began to play the new football game. In 1930, the first football world cup was played. Now everyone knows about football. Football for ever!

What a game!
Can I have a football, Mum?
Goal! Goal!
Football for ever! Football for ever!
Go! Go!

Index

ball 4, 18, 19
clubs 14, 16, 20, 22
England 6, 20, 22
game 2, 10, 14, 22
goal 4, 12, 18
players 12, 18, 19
rugby 16, 18
rules 10, 12, 14, 18, 19
Scotland 20, 22
soccer 16
team 12
world cup 22